REALLY EASY SAXOPHONE

FAVOURITE MUSICALS

CW00762894

WISE PUBLICATIONS
PART OF THE MUSIC SALES GROUP
LONDON / NEW YORK / PARIS / SYDNEY / COPENHAGEN / BERLIN / MADRID / HONG KONG / TOKYO

DOWNLOAD TO YOUR COMPUTER A SET OF
PIANO ACCOMPANIMENTS FOR THIS EDITION
(TO BE PLAYED BY A TEACHER/PARENT/FRIEND).
VISIT: WWW.HYBRIDPUBLICATIONS.COM
REGISTRATION IS FREE AND EASY.
YOUR REGISTRATION CODE IS KF924

ALSO AVAILABLE IN THE REALLY EASY SERIES...

REALLY EASY FLUTE MUSICALS
ORDER NO. AM998437

REALLY EASY CLARINET MUSICALS
ORDER NO. AM998448

REALLY EASY FLUTE FILM SONGS
ORDER NO. AM998481

REALLY EASY CLARINET FILM SONGS
ORDER NO. AM998492

REALLY EASY SAXOPHONE FILM SONGS
ORDER NO. AM998503

ALL TITLES CONTAIN BACKGROUND NOTES FOR EACH SONG PLUS
PLAYING TIPS AND HINTS.

PUBLISHED BY
WISE PUBLICATIONS
14-15 BERNERS STREET, LONDON, W1T 3LJ, UK.

EXCLUSIVE DISTRIBUTORS:
MUSIC SALES LIMITED
DISTRIBUTION CENTRE, NEWMARKET ROAD, BURY ST EDMUNDS,
SUFFOLK, IP33 3YB, UK.
MUSIC SALES PTY LIMITED
20 RESOLUTION DRIVE, CARINGBAH, NSW 2229, AUSTRALIA.

ORDER NO. AM998459
ISBN 978-1-84938-219-9
THIS BOOK © COPYRIGHT 2010 BY WISE PUBLICATIONS,
A DIVISION OF MUSIC SALES LIMITED.

EDITED BY OLIVER MILLER.
MUSIC ARRANGED BY PAUL HONEY.
MUSIC PROCESSED BY PAUL EWERS MUSIC DESIGN.

PRINTED IN THE EU.

YOUR GUARANTEE OF QUALITY
AS PUBLISHERS, WE STRIVE TO PRODUCE EVERY BOOK TO THE HIGHEST
COMMERCIAL STANDARDS. THE MUSIC HAS BEEN FRESHLY ENGRAVED AND
THE BOOK HAS BEEN CAREFULLY DESIGNED TO MINIMISE AWKWARD PAGE
TURNS AND TO MAKE PLAYING FROM IT A REAL PLEASURE.
PARTICULAR CARE HAS BEEN GIVEN TO SPECIFYING ACID-FREE, NEUTRAL-
SIZED PAPER MADE FROM PULPS WHICH HAVE NOT BEEN ELEMENTAL
CHLORINE BLEACHED. THIS PULP IS FROM FARMED SUSTAINABLE FORESTS
AND WAS PRODUCED WITH SPECIAL REGARD FOR THE ENVIRONMENT.
THROUGHOUT, THE PRINTING AND BINDING HAVE BEEN PLANNED TO
ENSURE A STURDY, ATTRACTIVE PUBLICATION WHICH SHOULD GIVE YEARS
OF ENJOYMENT. IF YOUR COPY FAILS TO MEET OUR HIGH STANDARDS,
PLEASE INFORM US AND WE WILL GLADLY REPLACE IT.

WWW.MUSICSALES.COM

CD TRACKLISTING

1 NO MATTER WHAT
   (FROM 'WHISTLE DOWN THE WIND')
   (WEBBER/STEINMAN)
   THE REALLY USEFUL GROUP LIMITED /
   UNIVERSAL MUSIC PUBLISHING LIMITED

2 ANY DREAM WILL DO
   (FROM 'JOSEPH AND THE AMAZING
   TECHNICOLOR® DREAMCOAT')
   (WEBBER/RICE)
   THE REALLY USEFUL GROUP LIMITED.

3 BEAUTY AND THE BEAST
   (MENKEN/ASHMAN)
   WARNER/CHAPPELL ARTEMIS MUSIC LIMITED

4 BREAKING FREE
   (HOUSTON)
   WARNER/CHAPPELL ARTEMIS MUSIC LIMITED

5 FOOTLOOSE
   (LOGGINS/PITCHFORD)
   SONY/ATV HARMONY (UK) LIMITED/SONY/
   ATV MUSIC PUBLISHING (UK)

6 HOPELESSLY DEVOTED TO YOU
   (FROM GREASE)
   (FARRAR)
   SONY/ATV HARMONY (UK) LIMITED

7 I JUST CAN'T WAIT TO BE KING
   (FROM WALT DISNEY PICTURES'
   'THE LION KING')
   (RICE/JOHN)
   WARNER/CHAPPELL ARTEMIS MUSIC LIMITED

8 I KNOW HIM SO WELL
   (FROM 'CHESS')
   (RICE/ANDERSSON/ULVAEUS)
   UNIVERSAL MUSIC PUBLISHING LIMITED

9 I'D DO ANYTHING
   (BART)
   LAKEVIEW MUSIC PUBLISHING
   COMPANY LIMITED.

10 IF I WERE A RICH MAN
   (HARNICK/BOCK)
   CARLIN MUSIC CORPORATION.

11 THE LAST NIGHT OF THE WORLD
   (SCHÖNBERG/MALTBY JR./BOUBLIL)
   BOUBLIL ALAIN OVERSEAS LIMITED

12 MAMMA MIA
   (ANDERSSON/ANDERSON/ULVAEUS)
   BOCU MUSIC LIMITED

13 ON MY OWN
   (SCHÖNBERG/BOUBLIL/NATEL/
   KRETZMER/NUNN/CAIRD)
   BOUBLIL ALAIN OVERSEAS LIMITED

14 THE RHYTHM OF LIFE
   (FIELDS/COLEMAN)
   CAMPBELL CONNELLY & COMPANY LIMITED.

15 A WHOLE NEW WORLD
   (FROM 'ALADDIN')
   (MENKEN/RICE)
   WARNER/CHAPPELL ARTEMIS MUSIC LIMITED

16 THE PHANTOM OF THE OPERA
   (WEBBER/HART/STILGOE/BATT)
   THE REALLY USEFUL GROUP LIMITED

No Matter What

Words by Jim Steinman • Music by Andrew Lloyd Webber

On 20th December 1998, one million music fans phoned ITV for this, their Record of the Year. It is taken from Andrew Lloyd Webber's successful musical, *Whistle Down The Wind*.

Hints & Tips: Aim to keep the long notes in tune, this is made particularly difficult when crossing from the low to the middle register, so practise the large intervals.

JOSEPH AND THE AMAZING TECHNICOLOR® DREAMCOAT

Any Dream Will Do

Words by Tim Rice • Music by Andrew Lloyd Webber

Released as a single in 1991 by Jason Donovan who was then playing Joseph in the West End production of the musical at the London Palladium, this song topped the UK charts for two weeks. In 2007 BBC TV ran a series, named after the song, searching for a new Joseph, a role eventually won by Lee Mead.

Hints & Tips: This piece is a good study for playing in the upper register, but don't let it go sharp or out of tune, particularly at bars 25-26.

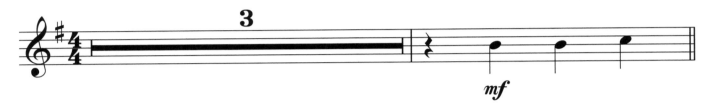

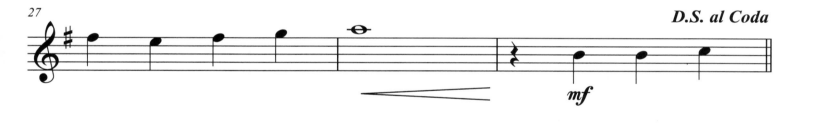

Beauty And The Beast

Words by Howard Ashman • Music by Alan Menken

Blending traditional animation with computer generated imagery, this is the only full-length animated feature film ever nominated for an Academy Award for Best Picture and the first film ever to receive three Academy Award nominations for Best Song, from which this one, sung by Celine Dion and Peabo Bryson, became the Oscar winner.

Hints & Tips: Play this piece as the marking says, gently, and keep it smooth and flowing. Take particular care of the large intervals.

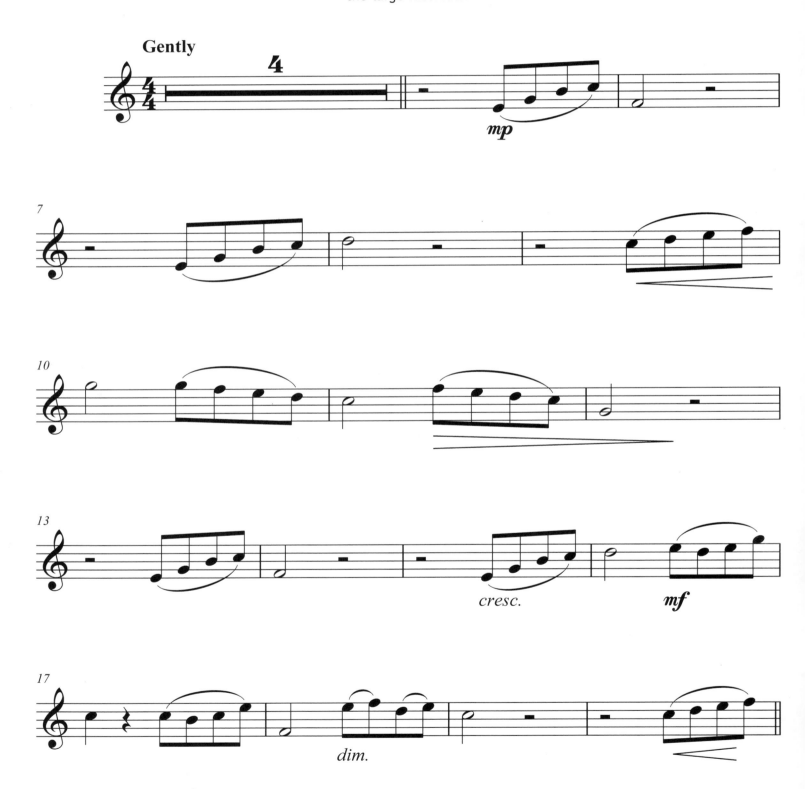

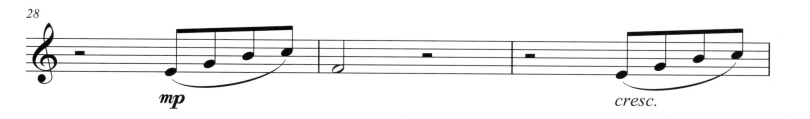

7

Breaking Free

Words & Music by Jamie Houston

At the climax of what the author describes as a modern adaptation of *Romeo And Juliet*, the main characters, Troy and Gabriella, audition for the winter musical in front of the entire school. Gabriella freezes when she sees everyone staring at her, but encouraged by Troy, she finds the courage to sing this song.

Hints & Tips: The staccato C in bar 16 is important to help phrase the music, so take care to play it accurately.

cresc.

f

mf

Footloose

Words & Music by Kenny Loggins & Dean Pitchford

This song opens and closes the musical, first performed on Broadway in 1998; a classic tale of repression and teenage rebellion in which streetwise city boy Ren helps revitalise the spirit of the small town of Bomont after a tragic car accident by persuading the townspeople to reintroduce dancing after a five-year ban.

Hints & Tips: Keep the articulation neat and crisp, particularly at bar 28 where the Cs need separating. The accents in bars 6 and 10 don't want to be too heavy, just stress them slightly.

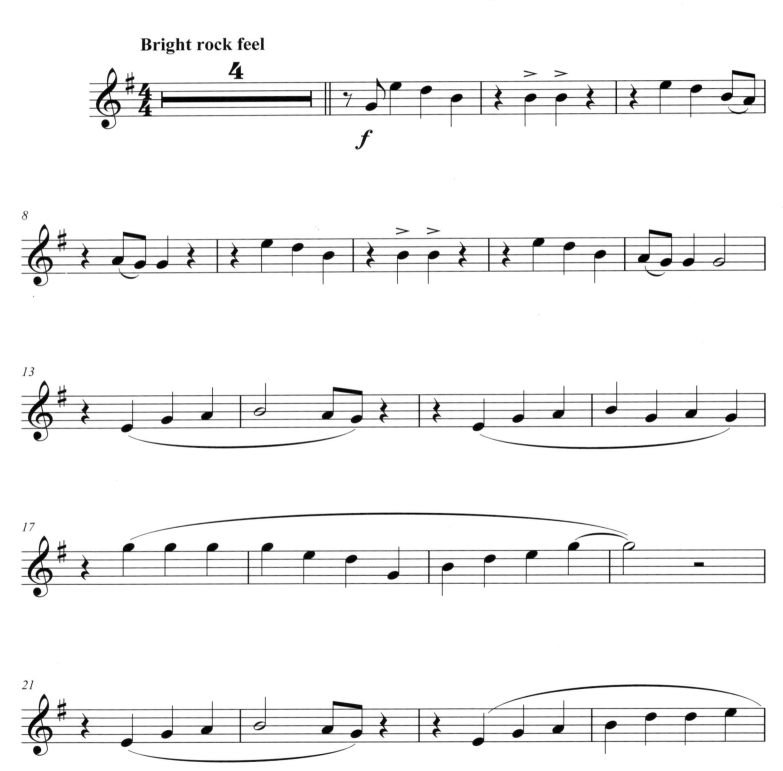

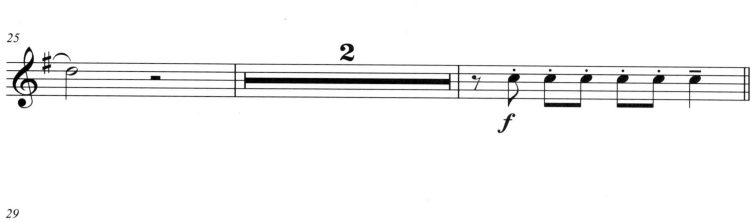

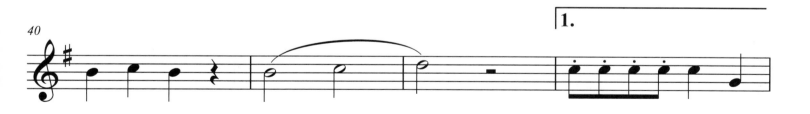

11

Hopelessly Devoted To You

Words & Music by John Farrar

Olivia Newton-John – who, incidentally, was up against Abba in the 1974 Eurovision Song Contest – just kept reinventing herself until she finally hit it big as Sandy in *Grease*. This was her unforgettable solo number.

Hints & Tips: Be ready for the key change at bar 41. Rather than thinking of the time signature as 6 semiquavers in a bar, try to think of it as 2 beats a bar for it to flow better. At the change of key signature use the Bis side key for B♭.

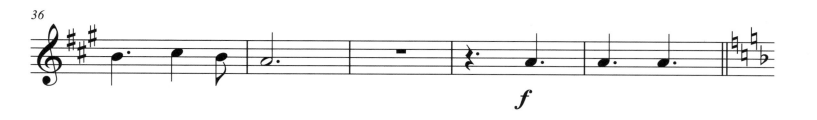

I Just Can't Wait To Be King

Words by Tim Rice • Music by Elton John

Lion cub Simba brags to his friend Nala about his future role as successor to his father as ruler of the Pride Lands as, although forbidden, they sneak off to the elephant graveyard. Based on a 1994 Disney animation of the same name, the musical, featuring actors in animal costumes and giant puppets, first opened in 1997.

Hints & Tips: D on the fourth line of the stave (concert A) is not a nice note to play on the alto saxophone, this piece will be a good test and therefore good practice for playing it.

I Know Him So Well

Words by Tim Rice • Music by Benny Andersson & Bjorn Ulvaeus

Elaine Paige and Barbara Dickson had a UK No.1 with this duet even before the musical opened in London in 1986. As with *Jesus Christ Superstar* and *Evita*, an album was released in advance, music this time by Benny and Björn of Abba, as lyricist Tim Rice's regular partner, Andrew Lloyd Webber, was busy with *Cats*.

Hints & Tips: Try playing the large intervals of the melody slowly, aiming to make a good sound and keep them in tune, which will help you to gain flexibility and attain greater accuracy when playing at the correct speed. Be light with all staccatos.

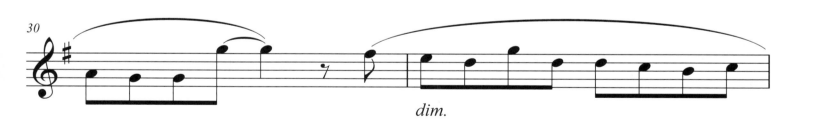

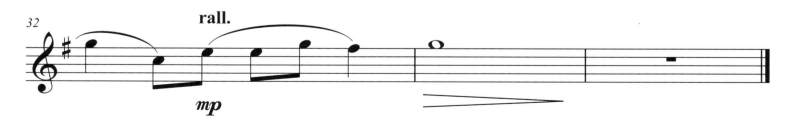

I'd Do Anything

Words & Music by Lionel Bart

The BBC chose the title of this song for their 2008 TV series, eventually won by Jodie Prenger, in which they searched for a new, unknown lead to play Nancy, plus three boys to take turns to play Oliver, in a West End revival of the musical, based on Charles Dickens' 1838 novel *Oliver Twist*, which first opened in 1960.

Hints & Tips: Use the long or side B♭ key for A♯ at bar 8: B♭ and A♯ are the same note, they are called enharmonics.

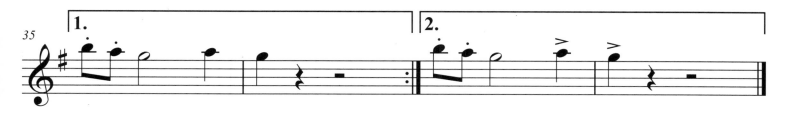

If I Were A Rich Man

Words by Sheldon Harnick • Music by Jerry Bock

A story about a philosophical dairy farmer, Tevye, played by Topol in the film, who strives to maintain traditional Jewish values in the face of oppression from the Tsarist Russian Orthodoxy. In this song Tevye wishes he was a man of leisure and influence in the community.

Hints & Tips: There are many accidentals in this piece – accidentals are sharps (♯), flats (♭) and naturals (♮) which don't appear in the key signature, so take care that you're playing the correct notes. Be light with the staccatos.

The Last Night Of The World

Words by Richard Maltby Jr. & Alain Boublil • Adapted from original French words by Alain Boublil
Music by Claude-Michel Schönberg

Miss Saigon was inspired by the same play that inspired Puccini to write *Madama Butterfly*. To date the show has been seen in 138 cities worldwide.

Hints & Tips: This is another piece with lots of accidentals to watch out for. Don't take a breath at the quaver rests in bars 38 or 39 otherwise you might come in late, try to get from bar 37 to the crotchet rest in bar 41 in one breath.

Mamma Mia

Words & Music by Benny Andersson, Stig Anderson & Björn Ulvaeus

This stage musical, which opened in London in 1999 and on Broadway in 2001, takes its title from Abba's second UK No.1 hit. It topped the charts for two weeks early in 1976, nearly two months after its release, replacing Queen's 'Bohemian Rhapsody', another song which includes 'mamma mia' in its lyrics!

Hints & Tips: There are many repeated notes in this piece (bar 21 etc.) so take care that they are even, that none are more prominent than each other.

On My Own

Words by Herbert Kretzmer, Trevor Nunn & John Caird • Original French Words by Alain Boublil & Jean-Marc Natel
Music by Claude-Michel Schönberg

The lovestruck Eponine sings of her unrequited love for Marius, the student revolutionary. Despite a warning, Eponine returns to the Barricade, is wounded and dies in Marius' arms.

Hints & Tips: A good control of the embouchure is needed for this piece. There are some tricky sections: when you play with the CD it feels faster than it actually is, so it would be useful to listen to the recording beforehand. Watch out for the accidentals in bars 11-13, and then the change of key at 19. Also note the time signature changes.

cresc.   *f*

ff

rall.

The Rhythm Of Life

Words by Dorothy Fields • Music by Cy Coleman

This musical, which opened on Broadway in 1966, follows the unlikely adventures of Charity Hope Valentine, a dancer at the Fandango Ballroom, New York, who gets stuck in a lift at the local YMCA with a claustrophobic accountant, who invites her to his Rhythm of Life Church.

Hints & Tips: There aren't many places to breathe in this piece! Try to take musical breaths, in places that don't disrupt the music, so not in the middle of a phrase, or a quick snatched breath if one must be taken. It is always useful to work out where you will breathe beforehand then practise the same breaths.

A Whole New World

Words by Tim Rice • Music by Alan Menken

Tim Rice took over as lyricist for the movie, based on the Arabian folktale *Aladdin's Wonderful Lamp* from *One Thousand and One Nights*, when Disney regular Howard Ashman died in early 1991. In 1993 this became the first Disney song ever to reach No.1 on the US Billboard Hot 100.

Hints & Tips: Keep this piece as legato as possible. It is easy to fall behind the beat, so try not to; be rhythmic. Relax the embouchure for the low Ds in bars 6 and 12.

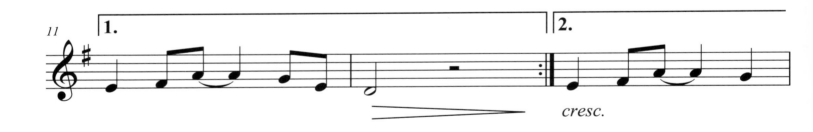

31

The Phantom Of The Opera

Words by Charles Hart • Additional Words by Richard Stilgoe & Mike Batt
Music by Andrew Lloyd Webber

This musical is based on a 1911 novel by French writer Gaston Leroux. The story concerns a composer whose disfigured face drives him to shun the everyday world in favour of the vast cavernous cellars of the Paris Opera.

Hints & Tips: When coming down from the high D in bar 19 keep the quavers rhythmic as it is easy to rush, making certain to hold the D for it's full length will help with this.

123456789